WORMS

Lois and Louis Darling

WILLIAM MORROW AND COMPANY   NEW YORK 1972

BY LOIS AND LOUIS DARLING
Before and After Dinosaurs
A Place in the Sun
Sixty Million Years of Horses
Turtles
   published by William Morrow and Company
Coral Reefs
The Science of Life
   published by World Publishing Company

BY LOUIS DARLING
The Gull's Way
Kangaroos and Other Animals with Pockets
Penguins
Seals and Walruses
   published by William Morrow and Company

FOR BETTY

Living things
are either plants or animals.
Worms are animals.

There are many kinds of animals other than worms,
for instance, cats, dogs, mice, people, deer, elephants,
frogs, fishes, snakes, birds, grasshoppers, crayfishes,
starfishes, jellyfishes, and others.

Cats, dogs, mice, people, deer, elephants, frogs,
fishes, snakes, and birds all have a backbone
as well as other bones that make up a skeleton,
which protects and supports their body.
Worms are animals that have no backbone or any other bones.
There are other animals that have no backbone—

grasshoppers, crayfishes, starfishes, and many more.

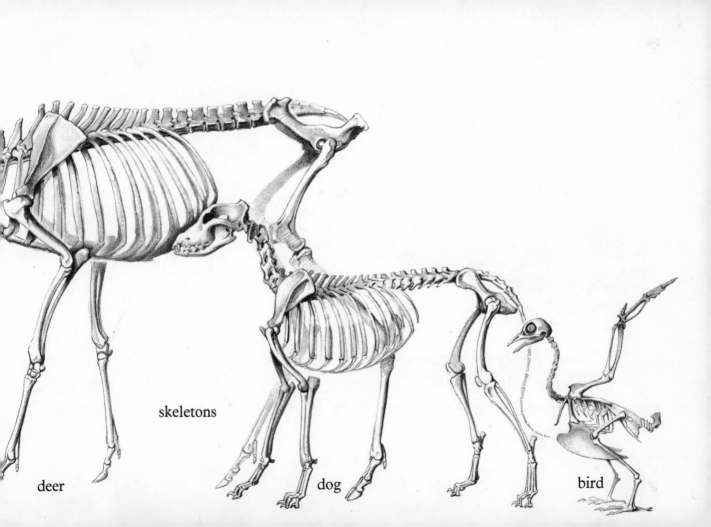

skeletons

deer

dog

bird

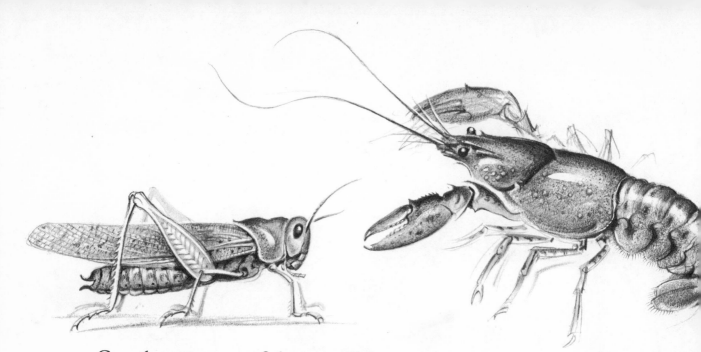

Grasshoppers, crayfishes, starfishes, and such
all have a hard outside covering

10   that protects and supports their body.

A hard outside covering would be no use to a worm.
Nor do they need a bony skeleton so they can live like you
or fly like a bird
or swim like a fish.
Each kind of animal lives its own kind of life
in its own kind of place.
Worms live in water or moist soil.

flatworms

There are many different kinds of worms—
flatworms, roundworms, horsehair worms,
and segmented (seg-*men*-ted) worms.
This book is about segmented worms.

12

roundworms

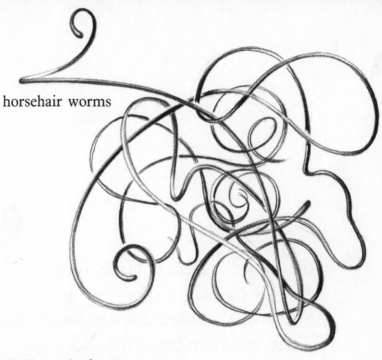

horsehair worms

Flatworms, roundworms, and horsehair worms
are not closely related to segmented worms.

There are different kinds of segmented worms.
Nereid (*near*-ee-id) worms are one kind that live in the sea.
Some of them are colored bright red, green, blue, or yellow.
They are very beautiful.
Their name comes from the old Greek tale
about the Nereids, who were lovely sea nymphs.

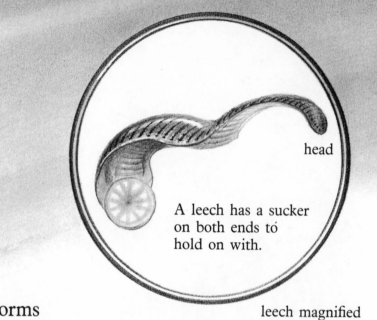

head

A leech has a sucker
on both ends to
hold on with.

leech magnified

Leeches are segmented worms
that live in water.
In some tropical countries they also live in damp places on land.
Leeches, too, are often beautiful with bright markings.

They swim swiftly through the water with a wavy motion.
You sometimes see them in ponds, lakes, and rivers.
Usually, however, they swim about at night,
resting and hiding in the daytime.

Earthworms are also segmented worms.
Some are very small; some are large.
In Australia there are earthworms
from four to twelve feet long.

Most of the worms you see,
like those that robins eat and fishermen use for bait,
are only a few inches long.

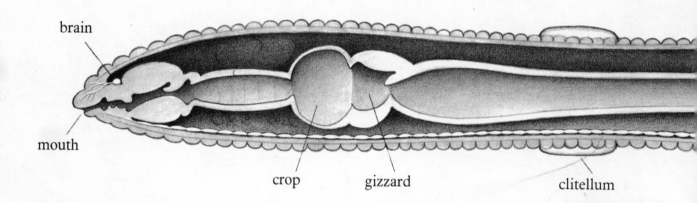

brain

mouth

crop

gizzard

clitellum

An earthworm seems to be a simple animal from the outside.
But it is not simple inside.
It has a digestive system made up of a mouth, a crop,
a gizzard, and an intestine.

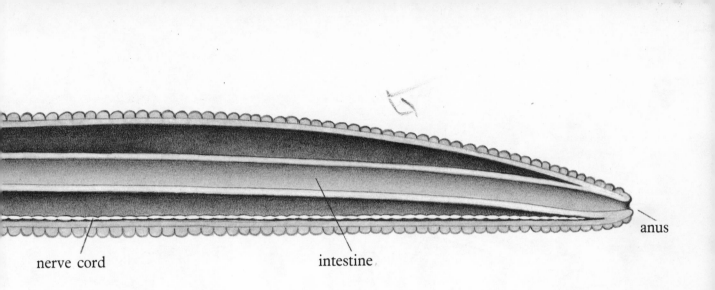

nerve cord

intestine

anus

It also has an outlet, or anus (*ay*-nus),
for wastes and leftovers from its food.
A worm has a brain and nerves that can collect messages
and send them to all parts of the worm's body.

21

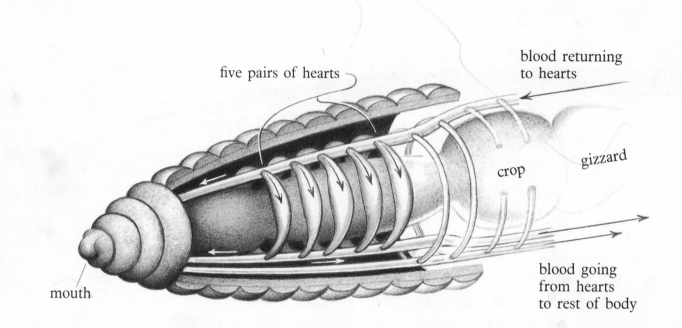

five pairs of hearts

blood returning to hearts

gizzard

crop

blood going from hearts to rest of body

mouth

Worms have a system of tubes, or vessels,
and five pairs of hearts that pump blood through the vessels
so that it can flow everywhere in the worm's body.
Worms have no lungs, nor do they need them.
Oxygen from air or water easily passes through
their moist thin skins into their blood vessels.

23

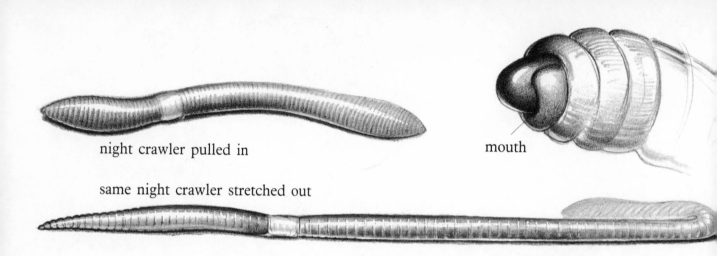

night crawler pulled in

mouth

same night crawler stretched out

Worms have strong muscles with which they can swell up,
thin down, stretch out, or pull in.
Worms do not have eyes, but they can tell light from dark.
They usually live underground during the day
24   and come out of their tunnels only at night.

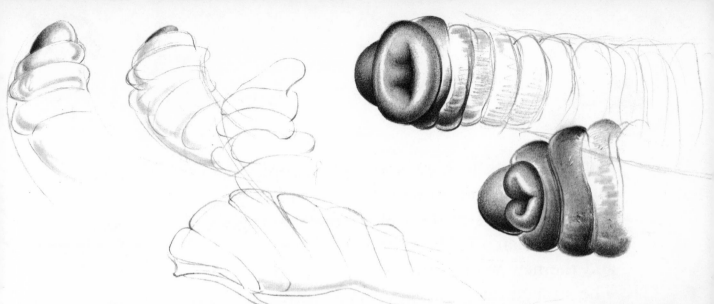

Although worms do not see, smell, or hear as you do,
their sense of touch is good.
They feel the smallest vibrations in the soil at once.

Cats give birth to kittens, dogs to puppies, humans to babies,
but worms do not give birth to wormlets.
Worms lay eggs in the soil in small packages called cocoons.
The eggs hatch in the soil,
and the new worms grow up by themselves.
The strange thing is that every earthworm
can be a mother and a father.
Every earthworm can lay eggs.
Every earthworm can mate with any other earthworm,
and produce eggs that will hatch.

clitellum

cocoon

After an earthworm has mated,
a cocoon is formed by the clitellum.
With the eggs inside, it slides forward off the worm's head.
The ends of the cocoon now close,
and one or more eggs develop.
They hatch from the cocoon as tiny wormlets.

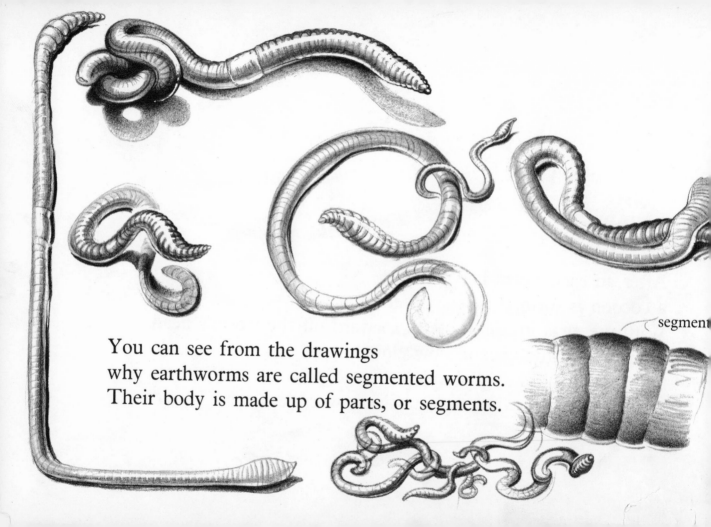

segment

You can see from the drawings
why earthworms are called segmented worms.
Their body is made up of parts, or segments.

Among worms the segments
are much alike from one end to the other.
Many other animals
also are made up of segments.
But their segments are not at all alike.

You would not think that any animal as smooth and slippery as an earthworm has stiff bristles on it.
But earthworms do have bristles,
although they are very, very small,
and there are only eight on each segment.
This feature is why earthworms belong to the class, or group, called oligochaete (*oh*-lig-oh-keet) worms.
Oligochaete is a word made up of two Greek words,
oligo, which means *few,*
and *chaet,* which means *bristle.*
So the word means *few bristles.*

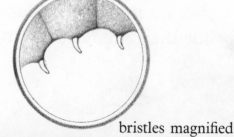

bristles magnified

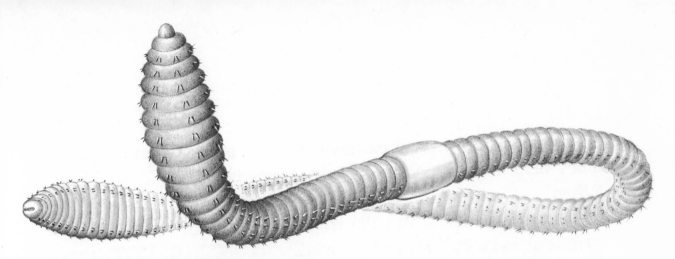

A name like oligochaete seems hard to say and remember.
But oligochaete is a good name in two ways.
1. It tells that this kind of worm has bristles, but only a few.
2. Scientists all over the world know what oligochaete means.
They can understand each other
no matter what language each speaks.

The few bristles that an earthworm has are very useful.
They help make it possible for it to crawl.
When a worm moves,
it starts by stretching out the front part of its body,
so that it is long, thin, and pointed.
Then it swells up the front part
and holds this section in place
with the help of the bristles on it.
Next the worm pulls in the bristles
on the back part of its body and pulls it up.

Now it stretches out the front part again and reaches forward again—

and so on and on and on.
Sometimes a worm makes all these movements in reverse,
so that it goes backward instead.

This way of crawling seems clumsy,
but worms move along fast when they are in a tunnel.
It is harder for them to move about outside,
where they do not have the sides of the tunnel to cling to.
Worms come out of the ground at night to find food.
Usually they keep the rear end of their body in the tunnel.
To reach food, they stretch as only worms can stretch.

If danger comes, they pull back into the safe tunnel quickly.

In loose soil worms make tunnels by pushing earth aside.
In hard-packed earth they form tunnels
by swallowing the soil,
passing it through their digestive system,
and leaving it outside the entrance.
If you look through the grass or in soil near worm tunnels,
you can see the pellets of earth
that worms have brought to the surface.

They are called worm castings.

worm castings

Digging tunnels is useful for worms.
There are bits of plant and other food mixed in the soil.
The worms digest this food
as the soil passes through their body.
They get a good part of their meals in this way.

Worms can breathe through their skin only when it is moist.
So worms stay underground,
except at night when the air is cool and damp.
If they are caught out in the sunshine
they quickly dry up and die.
When the top layers of the soil become dry in summer,
worms burrow deeper.
By midsummer it is often impossible to dig up a worm.

But in spring and fall the surface soil is full of them.

In winter, worms plug up their tunnels
and go deep once more.
There they curl up until the world is warm again.

In the rainy spring and fall
worms can be dug in garden or woods.
Manure worms can be found in manure piles on farms.
Big night crawlers can be hunted and caught at night.
With red plastic covering a flashlight lens, you sneak along
and spot the shine of a worm in the grass.
If you move softly and reach quickly,
you can catch it before it snaps back into its tunnel.
The worm often has a strong hold on the sides of its tunnel.

If you pull steadily, it soon will tire and let go.

Do not pull too hard.
You may find yourself holding only part of a worm.
If you let this front part go, it may live, grow a new tail end,
and become a whole worm again.
But the back part will not grow into a new worm.
Night-crawler hunting is a good way to get fishing bait,
and an exciting way to get better acquainted with worms.

Keeping many large earthworms alive for long is hard.
They need a large container filled with the right soil—
a mixture of loam, rotting leaves, and leaf mold.
This soil must be kept moist, but not soggy.
Large earthworms usually are kept only at worm farms
or at zoos to feed such animals as platypuses.
If you want to keep worms for a few days,
put them in a glass jar or a plastic container.
Half fill it with moist leaf mold or loose earth.
Put on a lid with a few holes in it and keep in a cool place.

platypus

Small white worms are used
to feed aquarium fishes, newts, frogs, and turtles.
They are called white worms, or enchytrae (*en*-ki-tree),
and are easier to keep than large worms.
A stock of them can be bought in most pet shops.
Fill a large glass jar (at least gallon size)
or a plastic pail almost full of moist leaf mold.
Put the stock of white worms in it and keep it in a cool place
with a sheet of glass over it to keep the moisture in.

Feed the worms every few days
with a little bread soaked in milk or with moistened pablum.
Dig these foods in below the surface an inch or two.
Never let too much collect and spoil.
The white worms will multiply,
and you will have a supply of live pet food all winter.

Earthworms are plentiful all over the world
wherever the soil is moist.
In one acre of good soil there may be three million worms.
These worms can bring as much as twenty-five tons of castings
to the surface every year.
In especially good soil there may be enough worms
to bring up thirty to forty tons of castings every year.

Worms change the soil greatly as they tunnel it, swallow it,
and deposit it on the surface as castings.
They stir and mix it as they bring deep soil to the top.
Worms cannot swallow stones,
so the soil they bring to the surface is fine.
Stones and coarse soil on the surface are slowly buried.
In thousands of years the buildings of long-ago cities
have been buried, partly because of worms.

As all this soil passes through the worms' digestive system,
it is enriched with wastes from the worms' food.

Worm castings bury dead plants and seeds.
When the dead plants are buried,
they enrich the soil even more as they decay.
When the seeds are buried they can sprout and grow.

This seed is sending forth a root.

seedling

Worms' tunnels help let air and rain seep into the soil
and keep it full of oxygen and moisture.
What is left over from leaves and other parts of plants
that worms pull down into their tunnels for food
also enriches the soil.

A worm pulls a leaf
into its burrow tip end first.

You can make an experiment.
Find the entrance of a worm's tunnel by its castings.
Put some green grass or leaves nearby for food
and cover the area with a box.
If you look under the box every day or two,
you will see that the growing piles of castings
form strange and beautiful shapes.

As the plants that worms pull beneath the surface
mix with the soil and enrich it,
they also help to make it loose and spongy,
so that water will trickle into it easily and be held in it.
Then when hard rains beat down upon the earth,
the soil will not wash away.
It will soak up the rainwater.
The soil will stay moist so that plants can grow in it.
Extra water will run into wells, springs, rivers, and lakes,
and keep them full.

All these things that worms do
to change the soil make it better soil.
Worms mix it and enrich it with plant parts and minerals.
Worms bring deep soil to the surface in their castings.
Worms make the soil spongy and loose,
so that air and water can get into it.
All these things make better soil
for the growth of the plants that cover this green world.
If worms did not do all these things,
plants would not grow as well;

in fact, many might not grow at all.

Both plants were
the same size before
worms were kept
in right-hand pot.

Plants are necessary to all other life on earth.
They are important in many ways that you can easily think of.
We get lumber from trees and clothing from cotton.
Plants cover the land and help keep rain from washing it away
or strong winds from blowing it about.

Plants, from the smallest bright flowers
to the great trees that cover the hills and mountains,
are also very beautiful.
And plants provide oxygen and food—
for everything else that lives.

If you think for a moment,
you will realize that every animal alive
can live only by eating plants,
or by eating some other animal that eats plants,
or by eating some of both—as you do.
So if worms are important to plants,
and plants are important to animals,
worms are important to animals also.
Because you are a human and humans are one kind of animal,
worms are important to you.

How worms affect your life is easy to understand.
Grasses and flowers grow in a meadow.
They are healthy, because worms help to make the soil healthy.
The grass is mowed for hay. It makes rich and nourishing hay.
The cows that eat the hay provide nourishing milk and meat.
People who eat and drink nourishing milk and meat
are likely to be strong and healthy people.

Worms play an important part in this cycle.
In fact, all the worms underneath a meadow
may weigh far more
than all the cows on top of it.

Of course, other living things are helped by the work of worms.
Grain grows better in soil enriched by worms.
Chickens that eat better grain lay more and healthier eggs.
Beans, peas, lettuce, carrots, onions—all sorts of vegetables
grow better in gardens where worms are plentiful.
Trees grow bigger and faster in soils that are rich with worms.
Flowers are more beautiful because worms live in the garden.
The lawn at home or in the park is greener
because of worms that tunnel beneath its sod
and bring their castings to the surface.

Everywhere the land and the living things upon it
depend upon those small and slippery animals
that live in the dark, moist soil—
the earthworms.